Build Your Authors Alley

A Convention Guide

Weston Kincade

Acknowledgements:

Thanks go to my editor Brandy Yassa and good friends Tavis Potter, Melissa Stasko, Pan Satyr, Laptop, James O. Barnes, Giggles, Marcus Calvert, and so many more at Cleveland ConCoction and in the convention circuit. They welcomed me into the volunteer fold. Their help was invaluable in making the most of Authors Alley, and I can't believe the wonderful comments attendees have offered about the event each year. Thank you. Speaking as a fan, volunteer and an author, we couldn't do it without you.

Disclaimer: This book is a work of nonfiction. All events and content within are the opinions of the author, who makes no guarantees to their effectiveness.

Copyright © 2018 by Weston Kincade

Originally published in 2018 in the United States of America by Amazon and CreateSpace.

All rights reserved, including the right of reproduction in whole or in part in any form.

For information about special discounts for bulk purchases, please contact Weston Kincade at weston@kincadefiction.com.

Book Editing by Brandy Yassa

Cover Art Copyright © 2018 by Simon Critchell

The text for this book is set in Cambria.

Manufactured in the United States of America

Summary: Have you ever wanted to organize a literary department? Maybe you already do, but it needs updated for the modern publishing world? But how? Now you can, with the help and expertise of best selling author and Authors Alley founder, Weston Kincade. Weston created Cleveland ConCoction's Authors Alley in 2015, and since then the convention regularly draws thirty active authors to participate annually. Panelists range from Nebula, Hugo, Elgin, Robert A. Heinlein, and Bram Stoker award winners to USA Today and New York Times best sellers. Panel and convention attendance has grown steadily every year. Weston Kincade has been contacted by conventions states away seeking advice, and other conventions are adopting the model with success. Now it is available to you in this short how-to guide, *Build Your Authors Alley*.

Inside, Weston provides detailed instructions to navigate you through the entire process. As an extra bonus, he has opened his toolbox of scheduling templates, example emails, newsletters, and a post-convention sales template to easily track your participating authors' sales.

To find your own convention success, pick up *Build Your Authors Alley* today.

ISBN 9781986218344 (Print)

ASIN B07B8X6XKH (ebook)

Table of Contents

Part I 1
   Backstory 3
Part II 7
   Publishing Expectations and Red Flags 9
   Convention Space 11
      Convention Green Room 12
      Authors Alley 13
      Literary Panel Room 14
      Why Not the Vendors Hall? 15
   Panelist Registration Packets 16
   Panels, Presentations, and Workshops 17
   Publisher/Editor's Tables 18
   Panel Sign-Ups, Registration, and Announcements 19
      Developing Registration Sign-Ups 20
      Researching Local Authors 21
      Contacting and Recruiting 22
      Biographies 23
      Panels 24
      Contacting Moderators 33
      Hotel Room Block Announcement 34
      Writing Newsletter Descriptions 35
      Guests of Honor Contracts 36
      Networking 38
   Staffing 39
   Hours of Operation 41

- Technology Needs 43
- Post-Convention Sales Reports 44
- Marketing 46
  - Social Media Marketing 47
  - Physical Marketing 48
  - Paid Marketing 49
  - Book Release Events 50
- Code of Conduct 51

Part III 52
- Table Costs 54
- Fighting Tradition 55
- Pick Your Battles 56
- Book Sales 57
- Book Vendors 58
- Competition 59
- Convention Problems 60
  - Facilities 61
  - Panel Problems 62

Conclusion 64
About the Author 65
Extras 66
- Links 66
- Authors Alley Email Examples 68
- Authors Alley Newsletter Example 75

Build Your Authors Alley

Part I
Intro to Convention Life

Build Your Authors Alley

Hello Reader,

If you are reading this, you probably have an interest in conventions and creating or updating the literary department of your local convention. If so, welcome! You are in the right place. First, a great big thank you for joining me in this adventure of convention life.

But who am I?

My name is Weston Kincade, better known for my Amazon bestselling A Life of Death trilogy and Priors series, but also for starting Cleveland ConCoction's Authors Alley. As of writing this, we are heading into year five of the convention and each year attendance seems to grow and grow. We regularly have thirty authors participating in three or more panels throughout the weekend. Most panels have four or five authors of varying experiences; from Nebula, Hugo, Elgin, Robert A. Heinlein, and Bram Stoker award winners to USA Today and New York Times best sellers, even self-published and first-time authors. Although ConCoction hasn't been around that long, I have been contacted by other conventions asking how I did it, seeking advice. Additionally, other conventions are starting to adopt the model for their own purposes. As a teacher by day, I take this as a compliment and would like to help.

There are many different factors that go into developing a literary department for a convention, which vary based on geographic location or other influences. Due to this, some of the things I've done may work better for you than others, and a few may work better with small tweaks. However, to start your literary department (what I call Authors Alley throughout this book) you need to have a good foundation. It is for this reason that I wrote *Build Your Authors Alley*. This is not a guarantee that your literary department will run perfectly, but it should give you a great start to creating one that is both fan and author friendly. Considering that the publishing industry has changed drastically over the last twenty years, having a good understanding of both volunteer life and publishing expectations is very important to a successful convention experience.

Build Your Authors Alley

Thanks again for joining me. If you have questions or concerns, I can be reached at weston@kincadefiction.com.

Weston Kincade

Backstory

As a hybrid author (published both traditionally and self-published), I encountered a great deal of problems with the way things are done in the publishing industry. And I am not alone. These are not intentionally kept secrets, but some might say they are secrets of the craft because most people have no idea they exist. I didn't until I started down the publishing road. Experience was my teacher, as is the case with many crafts and professions. However, in the modern day of publishing where self-publishing has become a much more viable option, it has allowed many authors to take control of their writing careers and find their audience. How do you accomplish this though? How do you get your books into the hands of more readers? That is the question that drove me straight into con life.

As people in the industry will tell you, publishing is changing. For most writers, the days of publishers footing the bill for marketing while the author works on his or her next bestseller are long gone. Your name is your brand. Both self-published and traditionally published authors are discovering that if they don't market themselves, no one else will. This can include giveaways, interviews, promotions, advertising, book tours and more. Enter, the convention circuit.

When I first moved to Cleveland, Ohio, I had already written and published four novels, co-written a short story anthology, published a few short stories in independent publishers' anthologies, and even ran a boutique editing agency for a host of authors, all while teaching during my day job. I was searching for another way of marketing myself. Friends in the Chicago area recommended that I participate in the new convention just starting in Cleveland called Cleveland ConCoction. Prior to this I hadn't been to a convention since college, where I attended TechniCon in Blacksburg, Virginia. TechniCon was a gaming convention, and I always enjoyed roleplaying there. However, this was a different adventure. ConCoction was coming up in a few days, so I grabbed my box of books and set off on a journey of discovery. I intended to meet the authors participating in panels and book signings, and also the volunteers running the event. I had no idea how best to even get into the convention circuit, let alone what to do, so I set out to see what I could learn. Little did I realize what was in store.

I showed up on Saturday, purchased a one-day registration, and searched the agenda for author panels or a Green Room where I could meet those in attendance. While there wasn't much, I did find one panel later in the evening and a room upstairs dedicated to attending authors. I set out to find the authors' room at once and discovered… an empty room. There were chairs and tables, but not one author was present. Figuring they must be participating in panels or grabbing lunch, I took a seat and waited. This decision proved invaluable, but not for the reason you would think. Time passed. I waited and waited. Finally, one gentleman arrived with a full book tote in hand and introduced himself as James Barnes of Loconeal Publishing. We spoke for a few minutes, exchanged information, then he left. The waiting continued. After about an hour, an independent author arrived with the same thing in mind as myself, to meet other authors in attendance, and we spoke a bit before he too left. It was becoming clear that something was wrong.

Ultimately, the time for the lit panel neared. I headed back downstairs to see if I would have better luck where authors were obligated to participate on panels. Attendees and myself gathered outside the room, waiting for the doors to open.

After a few minutes, security arrived, opened the door, and asked the crowd, "Could the authors please raise their hands?"

In that moment you could hear crickets chirp. I glanced around, much like the other attendees, but no hands stood over the crowd. Thinking quickly, I hesitantly raised mine.

"Great," he barked, motioning me forward. "Just you?"

After a quick explanation that I wasn't supposed to be running the panel, he shrugged, said, "It's all yours," and walked away.

Build Your Authors Alley

I was astonished, but now the crowd was staring at me. Leading them into the large banquet room, I introduced myself and took the stage to talk about my books and experiences. The panel went well, considering it was completely improvised, and I followed up with a Q and A session. None of it was planned or orchestrated, for I hadn't even met the convention volunteers, aside from security, but my experience speaking in front of classes allowed me to slip into the role.

An hour later, when the audience filed out and the high of speaking in front of strangers began to dwindle, it occurred to me what I had done. I didn't know anyone here, and no one knew me. I was new to the city itself, even. And I had *hijacked* a panel to market my books. While I didn't know how bad this would be perceived, for I had no idea about the workings of volunteer conventions, I was pretty sure it wasn't supposed to go this way. I needed to create a good impression with these people and I might have just killed any chance I had, so I set off to find the volunteers in charge and confess my sins. The only thing I had to guide me was a name, but not even a real one. My Chicago friend volunteered in similar circles and had given me the convention chair's name, someone called Giggles.

Venturing into the Vendors Hall, I introduced myself to one volunteer who took me to another dressed in a leather outfit that could have been worn in any BDSM video. After explaining, she led me to the aforementioned Giggles. To my surprise, instead of berating me for commandeering their panel when none of the authors showed, I was asked to head up the literary department for the following year. And so began my journey into planning and organizing Authors Alley for Cleveland ConCoction.

I had quite a few things working against me that first year. As I mentioned, I was new to the city, hadn't attended a convention in a decade, and had never attended one with a literary department, so I had a lot to learn. Since I had connections in the Chicago area, my old college friend Tavis agreed to go with me to a variety of conventions in the area to learn how best to set up what I coined "Authors Alley" at Cleveland ConCoction. And, yes, I am a fan of alliteration.

Over the coming months, Tavis and I attended three different conventions around northern Illinois. Each convention had a huge focus on supporting writers in their charters, and they had been running for decades. What surprised me most about each trip was that while I expected to find the best way to run Authors Alley, I really learned what not to do. That isn't to say that the conventions were failures or that what they were doing was wrong. In fact, they were great overall. I regularly return and assist them in various departments even today. However, what I learned was that each convention's literary department hadn't changed with the times. The publishing industry today is very different than it was thirty, twenty, or even ten years ago. Each convention I attended provided me with problems to work through, and my own experiences as an author would enable me to create an Authors Alley that was both author and fan friendly.

Armed with this knowledge, I decided to take advantage of my newest potential source: James O. Barnes of Loconeal Publishing, who I met in the author's room at Cleveland ConCoction. He had mentioned past experience attending and organizing literary departments at similar conventions. Fortunately, one email opened the door to a meeting and ultimately a friendship. James provided help, advice, and has been a huge part of ConCoction's Authors Alley ever since.

Now, four years later, Authors Alley is thriving, our volunteers are passionate about helping authors and readers, and around thirty authors participate annually. Panelists range from self-published and newly published to New York Times, Amazon, USA Today, and international bestselling authors. They include esteemed Bram Stoker, Hugo, Nebula, Elgin, and Robert A. Heinlein award winners, and some are included reading material on the International Space Station.

Part II
Convention Needs

When designing a convention, there are many things to keep in mind. Topics, demand, and the resources of your local area are enormously influential in determining whether your convention is a success. Does the demand exist for your convention? Have you come up with topics relevant to the people involved? And does your local area offer professionals in the industry of interest to draw people in? If you answered "yes" to these three questions, you have the makings of a great convention. If you don't know, then you have some research ahead of you. But assuming you have done that, it's now time to either update your current convention or create the convention most people dream about.

For this section, I will be covering:
- Publishing Expectations and Red Flags
- Convention Space
- Panelist Registration Packets
- Panels, Presentations, and Workshops
- Publisher/Editor Tables
- Panel Sign-Ups, Registration, and Announcements
- Staffing
- Hours of Operation
- Technology Needs
- Post-Convention Sales Reports
- Marketing
- Code of Conduct

Publishing Expectations and Red Flags

Publishing expectations have changed a great deal since e-books and self-publishing turned the industry on its head. This is a topic many readers and unpublished writers have questions about, and it makes a great panel topic. However, as a con organizer it is important to know the expectations and red flags of writing associations.

As the founding department head of Cleveland ConCoction's Authors Alley, when the convention board initially informed me that I had to charge author panelists for registration, I was hesitant. I am an author, and authors should not be charged to volunteer as a panelist when they draw many attendees to the convention. However, I had no ammunition to fight the decision and the responsibility fell on me to notify them when recruiting. Multiple authors contacted me in response. Some refused to attend when they saw that there was a charge, and I have not heard from them since. Others pointed out that the Science Fiction & Fantasy Writers of America (SFWA) and other associations forbade attendance or red flagged conventions that charged authors who participated in panels. Even though I'm a member of the Horror Writers Association (HWA), I fully admit that I do not know all of the policies of writing associations. But this was the ammunition I needed. It gave me the opportunity to come up with an alternate solution: a 5 percent fee tacked onto all book sales processed by Authors Alley volunteers. It would reposition the needed income for tables and facilities from the author to the customer. While not ideal, it was a small enough fee that I did not think convention attendees would balk since they were getting signed books and an experience that could not be purchased on Amazon.

The convention board agreed, I made up signs about the fee, and soon everything fell into place. During the first year of the convention when this fee was in place, attendees understood and were happy to pay it. Those I talked to compared it to the autographing fee other conventions charge. However, after 2015, Ohio changed the state laws regarding fees and taxes for non-profits, making the fee's legality questionable. As a result of this, and the very positive turnout in 2014, the board waived the fee in subsequent years.

So when you go to update or build your Authors Alley, keep this in mind and it may help overcome some hurdles and embarrassment.

Convention Space

It is important to keep in mind the demands of your panels and Authors Alley. The last thing you want is to have organized a wonderful convention but not have the space to accommodate furniture, panelists, and attendees. At Cleveland ConCoction we always have a minimum of two rooms, one designated as the Authors Alley and one for all of our literary panels. Each room needs to be at least twenty-five feet by twenty-five feet to accommodate everything. If you have the space and panelists to run two or more lit panels simultaneously, you could have more, but limitations on convention space have not allowed us to expand that much. In this section I will cover the following:

- Convention Green Room
- Authors Alley
- Literary Panel Room
- Why Not the Vendors Hall?

Convention Green Room

Conventions often do not have a room dedicated to panelists or authors. This is a problem on both counts. In fact, up to this point we haven't had room for a Green Room at Cleveland ConCoction, but every convention should if possible. The Green Room acts as a place for all panelists to go and escape the constant challenges of dealing with customers. Imagine a coffee lounge for employees. It serves the same purpose. Whether you are a performer such as a musician, cosplay presenter, celebrity, author, or panelist, a place to escape and just chat with other presenters between performances and relax is an enormous help. Seating, simple drinks, and edibles will make the most of this space.

Authors Alley

More importantly for literary departments, a room dedicated to authors is needed. This is not a Green Room. It serves as the authors' home base, providing shelving for their books, volunteers to sell their books when they are busy with panels and need breaks, and also gives your convention a wonderful place for authors to congregate and do book signings. Many story ideas have come from discussions between convention-goers and authors in our Authors Alley.

In Authors Alley, I generally have three to four extra-tall bookshelves (one shelf dedicated to each attending author); four to five six-foot tables (free use, first come, first served autographing tables, two to three seats at each); one six-foot table for swag, giveaways, and drawings authors might be hosting; and one six-foot table for the Authors Alley department head and volunteers to man (to sell authors' books for them when they aren't around). A check is sent to each author approximately one month after the convention for the total sales from the convention weekend. This requires close tracking of books provided by the authors for sales by the convention (the books on the bookshelves). ConCoction authors have a second set of books they keep on hand to sell from while outside of Authors Alley. Or, if they are manning a table in Authors Alley and make sales from their bookshelf, they will resupply the shelf to keep our numbers accurate. When an author checks in at Authors Alley, we count and input any adjustments needed to properly reflect how many of each book an author brings. We use Square's point-of-sale software for this. Also, a standalone/hanging chalkboard or monitor/tv advertising upcoming literary panels enables volunteers to quickly identify where authors are if convention attendees would like to buy a book when authors aren't present, hear them speak, and get them to sign it. This has also proven to increase panel attendance. Lastly, we keep two Square-enabled tablets in Authors Alley for tracking book sales, inventory, and taking credit cards.

Literary Panel Room

Many convention designers don't consider literary departments to be as much of a draw anymore. As a result, they will only have four or five author panelists and a few panels throughout the entire weekend. However, the last four years have proven to me and the department heads at Cleveland ConCoction that a literary track is certainly warranted. Many attendees come specifically for our literary panels, to meet and chat with authors, and to get books signed. Having a dedicated panel room where four or five panelists can sit at tables in front of the audience and speak about topics is essential. Each panel has a topic chosen ahead of time and one author who moderates the panel through questions and time management. Each panel lasts forty-five to fifty minutes, giving the upcoming panel ten to fifteen minutes for setup and to allow attendees to find their seats. An added benefit is that if you have designated rooms for your literary track and rooms for your other departments, it makes it easier for attendees to find panels they would like to attend.

Why Not the Vendors Hall?

I am often asked why Authors Alley at Cleveland ConCoction isn't in the Vendors Hall like many conventions. There are multiple reasons.

Initially, the separation was due to the size of convention space available at the hotel. Our Vendors Hall space wasn't large enough to accommodate the size of Authors Alley and the tables we needed. Another concern about having Authors Alley in the Vendors Hall came from the convention board. Exceptions would have to be made for the autographing tables since we don't charge for their use, but traditional vendors pay for their tables in the hall.

However, we discovered that having Authors Alley separate allowed us more individualized space to expand and incorporate book signings in Authors Alley itself, a different approach from conventions I attended previously. It does require directing traffic directly to Authors Alley. This can be accomplished through additional signage and specific directions in the convention program. We also chose a location that would funnel convention traffic from the Vendors Hall toward Authors Alley. This helped. Getting traffic can still be a problem, but having publishers' tables and signs in the hallway helps direct them to Authors Alley. If your Vendors Hall is large enough to have Authors Alley within it and your convention chair and department heads support your desire to update the program, give it a try. Having all purchases within the same large room might work well if facilities allow for it.

Panelist Registration Packets

    Registration packets should be picked up in Authors Alley rather than Registration. This will help panelists avoid lines or other mix-ups. For Cleveland ConCoction, what goes into the registration packet has evolved over the years from just a badge and program booklet to include the following:

- Badge, Holder, and Clip
- Schedule on a Postal Label (2" x 4" sticks to back of badge)
- Author Ribbon (to attach to their badge holder)
- Program Booklet
- Swag from Panelists and Sponsors (bookmarks, comic books, business cards, etc.)
- Name Tent (with their name on it for display in panels)

    Over the years we discovered that providing these proves helpful to our panelists and ensures the volunteers at Authors Alley have fewer problems to deal with. Feel free to make your own changes as you discover the specific needs of your convention.

Panels, Presentations, and Workshops

Depending on your experience, you may be wondering about the differences between a panel, presentation, and a workshop.

Panels generally have two six-foot tables upfront forming a row of seats where four or five panelists can sit, discuss, and speak to the audience. Depending on the size of the room, you may or may not need at least one microphone for a panel. Normally, panels will discuss a particular topic, with one panelist acting as the moderator to prompt the discussion with questions, maintain discussion focus, and manage time. In Authors Alley, this format has been expanded to include practice pitch sessions and advice on works in progress for attendees.

Workshops are generally where the audience participates and creates a product, much like your traditional classroom experience. In the past, we have had workshops on writing your first few pages of a book, short-story writing, character creation, and flash fiction. Often attendees will need tables to write on for workshops, so the layout is different from panels.

Presentations are the most traditional model. They normally include one or two people presenting to a room of attendees and often require a laptop and projector setup. Every year thus far at ConCoction, Hugo and Nebula award-winning science fiction author Geoffrey Landis has presented on the Mars Rover work he does at NASA. It is always well-attended, as is the Dr. Who presentation by Cindy A. Matthews.

At Cleveland ConCoction, we offer all three and encourage our panelists to provide new ideas when they register. The panel room generally works for all three so long as the equipment is ready ahead of time, but sometimes a workshop may have additional needs. In those cases, we generally try to schedule the workshop in an available room with more appropriate resources.

Publisher/Editor's Tables

Publishers and editors are a wonderful addition to a convention's literary department. They offer the potential for publishing deals to new writers, networking, and can participate in panels, offering a very different perspective from authors. What has proven even more successful in the past has been offering a pitch prep session, where attendees with a story idea can practice their elevator pitch and get advice from publishers and editors in the industry. Authors sometimes participate in this, too, on both sides of the table. During the convention, publishers can pay for a dedicated table where they sell books for all of their authors, just like they do in the Vendors Hall. However, because our Authors Alley is separate from our Vendors Hall, their tables should go inside Authors Alley or in the hallway just outside, increasing their traffic and helping to draw people in.

Panel Sign-Ups, Registration, and Announcements

What people generally don't see is what happens leading up to a convention. There are many things that have to be completed months earlier, including:

- Developing Registration Sign-ups
- Researching Local Authors
- Contacting and Recruiting
- Author Biographies
- Panels
- Contacting Moderators
- Hotel Room Block Announcement
- Writing Newsletter Descriptions
- Guest of Honor Contracts
- Networking

Developing Registration Sign-Ups

As you will see in Email Example 1 - Author Recruitment, a registration page is needed for participating authors to sign up. This is separate from convention registration, but it also provides the information needed to register the authors with the Registration department. We generally send a list of participating authors with contact information and badge info to Registration once the authors are finalized. This should generally occur no later than two to three months before the convention. It will give you enough time to finalize panel topics, schedule around authors' availability, assign moderators, finalize panel sign-ups, and advertise your authors prior to the convention.

To create this author registration page, I suggest using Google Forms. It's free and allows you to obtain everything you need. I have provided a copy of one of ConCoction's old registration pages as an example. Again, feel free to make use of what you would like in the survey and adjust it to your needs. Unfortunately, Google Forms does not let you make an actual copy of my draft (unlike with Google Docs), but you should be able to make use of it. Yes, it is a bit long, but every part serves a purpose that makes Authors Alley run smoothly for volunteers and authors alike. (See Authors Alley Registration Form in Extras.)

Researching Local Authors

When you are just starting out, researching local authors is incredibly important. I suggest researching them online. Most authors have websites with contact information. An additional way to find authors is through the other volunteers and fans. You can use social media and the convention site to inquire about new authors who might be interested in attending.

In subsequent years, researching will still be necessary, just not to the same extent. You want to try and get approximately 50 percent new author panelists each year so attendees don't always see the same people and books. If you are doing it right, you will see a large number of authors returning year after year. As you begin to deplete the area, expand your radius and research. In my experience, authors will travel from surrounding states to attend a good convention where their books sell well.

Contacting and Recruiting

Once you have the contact information for authors, as a convention volunteer in the literary department it's your job to recruit. That means contacting authors and inviting them to be panelists at the convention. (See Email 1 and 2 in Extras.) To do this efficiently, I recommend using Google Sheets to make a list of authors and their emails, then use the Yet Another Mail Merge (YAMM) add-on to contact up to fifty authors at a time using a Gmail draft. I have provided links to examples below. Please copy, paste, and adjust the emails to fit your needs. To see how, follow these instructions:

1. Follow the link to open the document
2. Go to the File menu and select "Make a copy…"
3. Give the document a new name
   - You can optionally share it with the same people as the original
   - Comments are not copied
4. Click "OK"

Biographies

Some authors have a tendency of sending extremely long biographies. This is a problem for conventions because program booklet space is costly. It isn't feasible for fan-run conventions (normally nonprofits) to dedicate a page or more to one particular author's biography. However, these lengthy bios are not that common. If an author submits one to you, feel free to ask them for a more concise biography. With fiction authors especially, they should have a short one available or be used to this expectation.

Panels

A great deal goes into developing and deciding on panels for a convention. Many people are involved, and working to accommodate more people makes the entire process even more difficult. By no means should you try and find a shortcut through this process though, because this is the content of your convention, the substance that people will be drawn to and base your success on. In the end, it deserves as much of your time as anything else, if not more.

For this section, I will be focusing on:
- Identifying Your Audience
- Panel Topics
- Choosing Panelists
- Scheduling Panels
- Panel Timing

Identifying Your Audience

Now, there are a few avenues to take when developing your convention's literary focus. The first thing to consider is this: is your Authors Alley geared more toward authors or readers? Yes, authors are readers, but readers are not normally authors. This distinction is important because their interests and reasons for attending conventions differ. Avid readers are often interested in finding their next great read, listening to their favorite authors talk about characters and stories, and discussing incredibly popular books and series. For instance, the most well attended and active panels I've seen at ConCoction and other conventions deal with what I call "staples of the industry."

The Dr. Who panel led by Cindy Matthews, an avid Dr. Who writer, is always standing-room-only. Mrs. Matthews has been running the panel since year two, and every year it seems to grow more popular. At another long-running convention I attended when researching how best to set up ConCoction's Authors Alley, Jim Butcher's *Dresden Files* is a staple panel that attendees love participating in every year. And no, with staple panels it often does not matter if the author is attending as a panelist or not. I am sure if they are it will be very well attended, so much so that it should be in one of the largest rooms you can find in your convention space. At other conventions, I have seen Game of Thrones, Star Wars, Star Trek and other well-known stories that ventured into the written word draw similar crowds. One can never guarantee that these panels will be popular in your location, but it's a safe bet. You can get a better idea of which topics will go over best at your convention if you throw the question up on social media and get input from your attendees.

However, if your convention is geared more toward writers, then you may want to have fewer panels celebrating current stories and characters and focus more on panel topics and workshops that deal with the writing process. Both novice and experienced writers enjoy talking shop, and for writers who are expanding their literary chops, learning from experienced authors who have delved into areas of marketing or publishing they may not be familiar with can draw attendees of various experience levels.

At Cleveland ConCoction, we tend to walk a line through both worlds. About half our panels in a given year deal with panel topics for readers, some staples and others discussing the best and worst villains or the like. The rest are for the benefit of writers. For instance, a popular topic with panelists and readers alike is Common Mistakes in Publishing. For panels like this, it is great to have an editor and a publisher on the panel if possible. Another popular one is Self-Publishing vs. Traditional Publishing. Having authors from both sides of the publishing industry—and especially hybrid authors like myself—make this a wonderful panel to attend.

Another question to keep in mind is this: will you focus on fiction or nonfiction? At ConCoction we have had authors from both walks of life attend as panelists. However, since our convention is geared toward gaming, cosplay, science fiction, and fantasy, our attendees are generally drawn to fiction. Paranormal, horror, and most genre fiction authors do very well too, but nonfiction books tend not to. This could be due to a lack of salesmanship by those nonfiction authors who have attended, or it could have to do with the audience. I have never turned an author away based on their genre or type of writing, though. However, we do warn erotica authors that this is a family convention and overt visuals are to be avoided. Normally this does not pose a problem, though, due to cover art standards in the publishing industry.

With that said, there is most certainly a place for nonfiction writers in the convention industry. Literary Cleveland, another group here in the city, runs conventions annually that focus primarily on nonfiction, poetry, and short fiction. I have attended them and been quite happy. If you are creating or updating your Authors Alley in a convention centered on writing instead of genre fiction, there is a large audience.

When coming up with your panel topics, keep an open mind. Some ideas would surprise you, and they can come from anywhere. At the last convention meeting, friendly banter turned into a panel idea called the Author Thunderdome. It isn't fully fleshed out yet, but I picture a panel with authors debating writing methods and the like. It may go nowhere, or it may appear at Cleveland ConCoction in coming years. It will certainly appear on the registration page for authors to choose if they like.

Panel Topics

When it comes to choosing panel topics for your first year's convention, it can be a little daunting. If you've attended conventions with a large literary focus recently, it will be to your benefit. If you haven't or it has been so long that you don't remember popular panel topics, there are a few steps to keep in mind.

Panel topics are important. Not only will they draw convention-goers in, they will also draw panelists and authors. On the Authors Alley registration page you will see a variety of topics from past years. This is updated each year based on the popularity of previous panels, and panelists can choose from them or volunteer new ideas. Those that turn out to be the most popular with authors often tend to prove popular with convention attendees, so we use the initial picks from registration to populate the initial schedule. Unfortunately, not all panelists will be able to fit the panel into their scheduled availability, but if they want to sign up for panels outside their availability, the SignUp.com email (Email Example 3 in Extras) will provide that opportunity.

Choosing Panelists

When it comes to deciding who would be best as a panelist, we tend to go with published authors, editors, and publishers. However, there are a multitude of people willing to participate with interesting perspectives. Keep in mind the topic of the panel, but be willing to venture into new and related topics. We have had people in particular industries act as panelists even though they may never have published themselves. For instance, for panels dealing with audio books and online publishing services, we previously had Chris Miller, co-founder of Podiobooks.com. His contributions to the panels were outstanding. Podcasters and book narrators are also great additions for panels dealing with online and audio book publishing. For panels dealing with the paranormal, consider contacting your local paranormal investigation group. They can be wonderful panelists. Keep an open mind.

Beyond that, sometimes even knowledgeable fans can fill in if a panelist can't make it and you have advanced notice. While I have seen this done at other conventions, ConCoction generally has enough authors participating that some will fill in from Authors Alley if a panelist has to miss.

Scheduling Panels

When it's time to start scheduling panels, there are a few things to keep in mind. We always start with a Google spreadsheet outlining all the panel topics we created. These were originally taken from successful panels in previous years and recommended panels from participating authors. We then highlight which panels were popular amongst registering authors and begin scheduling panels according to the panelists' availability. (See Registration Form in Extras.) There are many ways to do this, but this is how we accomplished it at Cleveland ConCoction.

Keep the panels limited to three to five participants depending on your facilities. If the front of your panel room is wide enough to accommodate two six-foot tables end to end, you can comfortably fit five authors to a panel. Now, on a spreadsheet create a schedule hour-by-hour for the hours your literary side will be open down the left side. Treat each row as a panel block for each panel room you have running simultaneously. If you are organizing a fan-run convention like Cleveland ConCoction where you have other departments like Art Alley, Cosplay, Kids, Vendors Hall, etc. you can use as many columns as you need. Fill each hour block in with a panel. If you have multiple rooms, make sure a separate column is dedicated to each. For multi-day conventions, I recommend creating a new tab for each day. Keep in mind authors' availability when scheduling and avoid assigning panelists to back-to-back panels if possible, especially during meal hours. Add your participating authors in each panel cell. (See Weekend Panel List in Extras.)

Next, use SignUp.com to create a panel list based on this schedule. You will need to create an account to do so, but at the time of writing this, creating a SignUp.com account is free. Input the names of authors who volunteered for available panels and create five spots for each panel. This is where authors will officially register in open spots. It is also the first time they will see the actual panel schedule. Once it is complete, it will provide you with a link to send panelists to follow. This is essential for the email to author panelists.

Before sending this third email, you will also need to establish the moderators for as many panels as you currently have people assigned to. We normally assign moderators based on four things: 1) limiting one to two moderated panels per person (the fewer the better because moderating takes extra time to plan, organize, and run), 2) experience moderating gives me more reason to comfortably assign them to be a moderator once more, 3) if the panel was the brainchild of a particular panelist, I will normally assign them to be moderator because they tend to know how they would like the panel to run, 4) if someone registered and indicated that they didn't want to be a moderator. As additional people sign up for new panels, you will have to assign moderators so that each panel has one. I have included a copy of an email we sent in the past for your benefit (see Email 3 in Extras).

Once panelists have finished signing up and the deadline has passed, make sure to update the Weekend Panel List. It is often used for programming schedule fold-outs (common in conventions). Fold-out schedules do not contain panel descriptions but provide convention-goers an easy schedule to follow during the convention.

Finally, create an outline of the panel schedules for each room hour-by-hour. Add the descriptions of each and the authors below each panel. We do this final draft using Google Docs. The benefit of this particular draft is that it allows you to include the panel descriptions and the authors. This is also the schedule we use in the programming booklet. An example Final Panel Schedule can be found in Extras.

Panel Timing

When to schedule panels is very important. You can have the most entertaining panelists or presenters and if you schedule the panel on a weekday before five o'clock, it can become a desert, tumbleweeds and all. This is where your expertise comes into play once again. Consider how popular the panel topic is, the panelists, their schedules, and how many attendees made it to the panel in prior years if you have that information. This will help you determine when to schedule it. On weekdays, it's generally accepted that most convention-goers won't be able to attend until the evening. Many people work days. Additionally, avoid scheduling popular panels when many attendees will be eating or another department has a big event such as a musical performance. Try to accommodate convention-goers by limiting the conflicts they will encounter. One of the things I always hate most when attending a convention is if my favorite panels are all scheduled at the same time. This can really become problematic if you have multiple literary tracks running simultaneously, especially if they deal with similar topics of interest. For example, avoid scheduling a writing workshop on introductory chapters at the same time as a short story writing panel. Both are likely to be of interest to the same audience.

Contacting Moderators

Once you notify your panelists of their scheduled panels and moderating responsibilities, you should send an email specifically to them describing the responsibilities and expectations. Moderators are very important. They manage the session, keep panelists involved, ensure the discussion doesn't wane, monitor time, and offer questions to guide the panel. An example based on some we've sent in the past is Email 4 in Extras.

Hotel Room Block Announcement

While your convention's hotel room block should have been announced before this point, it is still important to remind your panelists and guests about upcoming deadlines. The last thing you want to deal with is a cancellation due to insufficient space in the hotel. So, send out an email reminding panelists about hotel room block deadlines a couple months before the convention. Email 5 in Extras is a good example.

Writing Newsletter Descriptions

Most conventions have fan followers who follow announcements using social media, convention email lists and the like. These generally contain information about upcoming events in all the departments, such as guests of honor, panelist announcements, and other events that may require convention-goers to submit something early. Often these will come out quarterly leading up to a convention. To save time, an Authors Alley Newsletter Example is provided in the Extras.

Guests of Honor Contracts

At Cleveland ConCoction, we have a volunteer dedicated to negotiating the contracts with guests of honor. Other conventions undoubtedly do this differently, but it reduces the amount each department has to deal with. As Authors Alley volunteers, we make recommendations for who we would like to try and get each year, but the final say comes down to one person and the convention board. The Guest of Honor Liaison typically begins this process very early on. In fact, as soon as the previous year's convention is over, they generally start contacting potential guests of honor. Some respond quickly, but others may have to be reminded due to delays. Signed contracts will need to be obtained before any announcements are made about attending guests of honor.

With Authors Alley guests of honor, we have had great luck speaking with the author's publisher. They will sometimes provide free copies of their latest book to give away or other things that are invaluable and can only be obtained at conventions like this. The author or their agent can normally put you in touch with the appropriate person at the publishing house to speak with.

Guests of honor at nonprofit conventions like ours generally aren't paid. Because it is a much more relaxed experience where they have fun rather than being run ragged like at many for-profit conventions, well-known authors and other celebrities will generally come for the cost of travel, hotel, and subsidized or reimbursed meals. However, each person is unique and has their own preferences. You won't know for sure until you contact their agent or manager.

Often guests of honor may want an additional hotel night before or after the convention so they aren't rushing to the event. This works well and can be greatly appreciated. It also allows them to attend post-convention parties like the Dead Dog Party, if your convention has one. This provides volunteers a great opportunity to hang out with guests of honor without worrying about demands on their time.

When the guest of honor arrives for the convention, see to their needs, starting with picking them up from the airport. The liaison will normally deal with this, but once they reach the hotel or convention space, it is your responsibility to make sure they are registered and know their schedule. This does not mean you need to dedicate someone as their personal slave for the weekend, but someone should be tasked with seeing to their needs and checking with them periodically, especially during book signings and events where they need to be behind a table or on stage for an hour or more. Ensure they have a drink before they start the event, and when scheduling, try not to assign them to back-to-back panels. Like with all panelists, make sure each person has time to eat and enjoy the con a bit. You want the guest of honor to enjoy the process as much as the panelists and convention attendees. If they like it, they will be more likely to return later and will tell others about their experience.

Networking

Networking is a task many people find arduous or simply don't understand, but it doesn't have to be difficult. When you network, you are simply getting to know new people in the industry. Authors, publishers, and editors—no matter who they are—are people. Just treat them respectfully like you would anyone else and build friendships. If you are running an Authors Alley, networking needs to become second nature. You will deal with people of varying levels of celebrity, and connecting with them on social media can prove beneficial down the road. You never know who is friends with someone else, whose recommendation could change your convention overnight, or what the future holds. However, if you are outgoing and friendly and maintain an online connection with your panelists, it can open unexpected doors.

Staffing

Authors Alley can run smoothly with as few as two people. However, it will be very difficult and the volunteers will be working consistently all weekend, not to mention the time needed to get everything ready leading up to the convention. I recommend having five people who can accomplish the necessary tasks such as social media blast, website updating, scheduling, attending convention meetings, writing up announcements for the program, distributing flyers, and maintaining email communication with authors and panelists. This can be broken into the following roles:

- Department Head - Communicates with panelists, delegates to the Second, and schedules panels.
- Second - Assists department head, passes information to Authors Alley personnel, and delegates unforeseen jobs within the department.
- Writer - Develops announcements and the program booklet to meet publication deadlines.
- Social Media and Website Specialist - Maintains website announcements and posts to convention's Facebook and Twitter accounts about upcoming convention guests.
- Gopher - Passes out flyers and contacts universities, restaurants, and other locations where flyers can be posted for the appropriate audience to see them.

Cleveland ConCoction runs from Friday through the early afternoon Sunday. Friday tends to be light, and two to three volunteers at a time can manage it. Each volunteer will work about four hours on Saturday, switching out periodically for breaks and to give others time to attend panels and performances. Sunday can be handled by three to four people. Quite a few sales come on Sunday when convention-goers set out to spend the remainder of their convention funds.

The reason I give approximate numbers is that the additional person is generally sent out as a gopher to get things that are needed and, on an hourly basis, to count the number of attendees in each literary panel. While we normally provide our moderators a questionnaire (see Panelist's Materials) to fill out after each panel, where they will provide counts and other information, I prefer having the information immediately. This also enables us to deal with problems that may arise during a panel instead of waiting to hear complaints after the convention is already over, at which point it is often too late. Panelists and attendees both will have left with a tarnished opinion of the convention, whether the convention is at fault or not. Seeing to the needs of all people in attendance should be a priority at any convention.

Hours of Operation

Deciding how early to open and how late to close can be difficult, especially if this is your first time organizing a convention. However, I can't just tell you to open at a certain time and close at another. It isn't so cut and dry because it depends on your audience. At the long-running conventions in Chicago and Columbus, convention-goers normally like attending panels in the morning and afternoon, but after dinner, attendance tapers off as people go to parties or head home. The crowd here in Cleveland is different. They generally get up late and stay up late. In fact, even though there are parties Friday and Saturday nights that are well attended, many attendees enjoy going to late-night panels. As a result, our literary track of panels runs during the following hours:

Friday - 12:00 pm - 12:00 am
Saturday - 10:00 am - 12:00 am
Sunday - 10:00 am - 2:00 pm

At Cleveland ConCoction, Registration opens at noon Friday morning and the convention ends Sunday at three. Starting our first panel Friday at one o'clock gives people time to register, settle into their hotel rooms, look over the panels, and make it to the first panel in time. Opening ceremonies are at five Friday evening, so we generally won't schedule a panel during that hour. Closing ceremonies run from two to three Sunday, hence why we end a little early. It gives us time to take down the bookshelves, signage, and close up for the weekend.

Authors Alley runs on a slightly different schedule:

Friday - 1:00 pm - 9:00 pm
Saturday - 11:00 am - 8:00 pm
Sunday - 10:00 am - 2:30 pm

While there are potentially people interested in making purchases late into the night, there is no reason to further exhaust the panelists and volunteers. If your convention attendees are more active in the morning, you might want to open earlier. You will likely have to play it by ear the first year and see what people want. You do not want to lose sales for your authors, but you also do not want to push the volunteers and panelists so much that they no longer want to come. It's a balancing act.

Technology Needs

When organizing your convention, there will be technology needs that come up. Depending on the acoustics and size of your panel room, you may need a microphone and speakers for the panelists. This can be done with one microphone shared between the panelists, but I would recommend having at least two, one for the moderator and one to share amongst the other panelists. If you have the resources, though, wearable microphones for all five panelists would be ideal.

At Cleveland ConCoction, we regularly have scheduled events like Geoffrey Landis's annual Mars Rover presentation. Events like this require a projector, screen, and may even need a laptop set up before the presentation begins. That is why we ask questions about technology needs on the registration form. Given that information ahead of time, you can contact the department in charge of technology and make arrangements. For us, this department is Operations.

Post-Convention Sales Reports

Since Authors Alley volunteers make sales on behalf of their attending authors, the transactions must be linked securely to one account. At ConCoction this is run through the convention's Square account. When authors check in and pick up their registration packets from Authors Alley, they also drop off books for the Authors Alley Library. These are sold on the author's behalf, and a check is sent after the convention to reimburse the author. Since this is on the author's behalf, tax reporting is the responsibility of the authors. Before authors leave for the weekend, they are to pick up any remaining books or they will be donated to the charity auction the following year. There is an inventory check that takes place for each author when they are leaving to track inventory and ensure authors leave with the appropriate number of each book.

After the convention weekend, an analysis of all sales is taken. The purpose of this is not only to make sure authors are reimbursed accurately for the books sold, but also for data purposes. Each year we can see trends and changes. It tells us what genres are more or less popular with our convention attendees and can inform us when making future decisions or changes to the convention. Before any checks are written, the Sales and Reimbursement Report must be sent to the convention board along with a Reimbursement Report. These tally the total books sold per author and tell the convention chair how much to send each author for reimbursement. Just remember to add your authors' addresses to your final Reimbursement Report so the checks are not delayed or lost.

Checks will normally be sent out four to six weeks after the convention. While it would be great to send them sooner, only convention board members can write checks out of the convention budget and this does not occur until all departments have sent in their Sales and Reimbursement Reports. (See Sales and Reimbursement Report in Extras.)

Next, emails should be sent to author panelists with an accounting of their total sales, total inventory provided, and the amount to expect in the reimbursement check. (See Email 6 in Extras.)

A benefit to sending this email announcement is that it gives authors the opportunity to question the sales report and inventory before any funds change hands. This is important because there are times in every retail environment where shrinkage occurs, and the authors may notice something in the sales report you or your staff misses. "Shrinkage" in retail terms is loss due to theft, damage, shipping, or for reasons other than sales.

However temporary, since the Authors Alley has taken on the responsibility of selling for authors when they aren't available, the convention must also take steps to eliminate potential shrinkage. Volunteers need to remain vigilant to avoid such instances of theft from happening. To help with this, I recommend not placing Authors Alley shelving anywhere near the entrance or exits. Additionally, never leave Authors Alley unattended and always input sales data into the Square system. This will help avoid inventory discrepancies, theft, and the like.

At Cleveland ConCoction, we have only ever had one instance of shrinkage and it was the difference of one book. The convention covered the cost, adding it to the author's reimbursement check. In the event that something like this happens, take steps to track down the responsible party but—more importantly—try to appease all people involved. The cost of one paperback is a small price to pay for a panelist leaving happy, telling their friends and fans about the positive experience, and returning in subsequent years. In fact, taking a negative experience like this and turning it into a positive at the cost of a few dollars can be the cheapest marketing you ever pay for.

Marketing

As most successful authors will tell you, marketing is very important. The same can be said for conventions, and it is best to make use of every avenue possible that reaches a significant portion of your audience. There are really four types of marketing I'm going to go over here:

- Social Media Marketing
- Physical Marketing
- Paid Marketing
- Book Release Events

Social Media Marketing

The most important type of marketing we have encountered is social media. Facebook, Instagram, Twitter, and other free services offer people around the world the opportunity to communicate and keep up with their favorite events. Use fan groups, a convention Facebook page, and other avenues to get your announcements out to the masses. We try to announce one to two authors each week leading up to the convention on Cleveland ConCoction's Facebook page, beginning a few months prior to the event. We also use these services to share images and announcements from other conventions and products that appeal to our audience. To help engage our audience, we often ask questions that prompt them to offer suggestions or ideas for future conventions. Think outside of the box when approaching social media as an advertising avenue.

Physical Marketing

In many cases, especially when you are trying to cater to a local audience, you still can't beat the benefits of physical advertising. Our convention generally has flyers up at local colleges, bookstores, libraries, comic book shops, game shops, and even restaurants and bars who cater to readers or gamers. Go where your audience is and ask if they'd be willing to post the flyer on a window or cork board. Sometimes offering to advertise for them on social media can help this along. Remember, quid pro quo.

We also have volunteers who attend other conventions in surrounding locales and states. They will often work a table that advertises the convention. Sometimes we even work out a deal where Cleveland ConCoction hosts a hotel party at their convention to help get the word out. Again, offering advertising opportunities in exchange to help both organizations market themselves is essential. (see Networking for more information.)

Paid Marketing

There are different forms of paid advertisement available, such as magazine ads, online banner ads, even ads you can pay for in local theaters. While we have utilized some of these, the results thus far haven't proven all that beneficial. You have to find the right magazine or website targeting your audience, pick an affordable package, and try some out to discover whether the cost is warranted. I suggest caution when considering paid marketing. There are some that I am certain can truly benefit a growing convention, but be selective. Do your research.

Social media has thrown their hat into the ring with paid marketing over the years. I sometimes find Facebook advertising useful with a book release, but because of its regional and interest targeting options, this could be a good method to advertise for your convention. Just be careful. Facebook advertising will use your money quickly, so research how best to set up your ads and consider doing a few cheap test runs until you get the hang of it.

Book Release Events

If you have been in the convention circuit for any time at all, you probably know that late-night parties are popular with attendees. They are often in the party wing of the hotel, and BarFleet commonly hosts them at conventions across the country. But did you ever consider a book release party?

In 2015, Raw Dog Screaming Press joined Cleveland ConCoction and sent quite a few authors as panelists. In addition, they scheduled a book release party for one of their authors and coordinated it with the convention. Unfortunately, the author had to cancel due to illness and wasn't able to make an appearance, but the party was one of the most entertaining and well-attended of the night.

We also schedule other coordinated releases with authors who attend as panelists. Be creative in coming up with events. It could be a party, breakfast, special workshop, prize drawing, or anything you can think of. The convention uses social media and their website to promote the release to their audience, and authors will often cross-promote. This is a great opportunity to help each other.

Code of Conduct

In modern convention life, a Code of Conduct is essential. Too many conventions either don't have a Code of Conduct or haven't enforced it in the past. This has resulted in improper treatment of sensitive situations and bad publicity for a number of conventions. If you are developing one department as part of a much larger convention, this Code of Conduct should already be in place. If not, take steps to put one together. Ashe Dryden has written extensively about this and offers a great deal of resources on her website, Programming Diversity (https://goo.gl/BaWpHh). Your attendees and panelists deserve to know there are expectations for how people should and should not act and that you are prepared to enforce those rules. That last part is the most important. The board needs to enact appropriate consequences when situations arise that keep all attendees safe and eliminate future situations from occurring within the convention.

Part III
Convention Hurdles

Build Your Authors Alley

When designing the literary side of a convention, there are a lot of hurdles to keep in mind. Conventions that have been running for years, even those with literary focused charters, are seeing a drop in attendees and—as a result—panelists. This is because these conventions generally focus on traditionally published authors from what are commonly known as the Big Five Publishers (Hachette, HarperCollins, Macmillan, Penguin Random House, Simon and Schuster). Typically, they have not updated their rules and procedures to accommodate the changing publishing landscape. Self-publishing and independent publishing houses now make up a very large percentage of book sales, and these publishers, editors, and authors offer a wealth of knowledge and entertainment to convention-goers. To keep up with modern publishing markets and enhance the convention experience, literary department heads need to adapt. Here are a few hurdles to keep in mind that I learned about over the last four years and had to overcome:

- Table Costs
- Fighting Tradition
- Pick Your Battles
- Book Sales
- Book Vendors
- Competition
- Convention Problems

Table Costs

Originally the board of Cleveland ConCoction didn't know how registration sales would do as a result of adding Authors Alley and panels. As a result, the first year they wanted to charge for the use of autographing tables and author registrations to the convention. Their policy to reimburse panelists who participated in three or more panels still applied, but this proved problematic when it came to writing associations and their standards for conventions.

To address author concerns and those of the convention board, I adopted an alternate method of reimbursement. Instead of charging for the use of autographing tables and convention registrations, I instituted a 5 percent fee for purchases through Authors Alley, which the board approved. This was simply to cover the costs that make the literary department possible. Fortunately, convention-goers did not seem concerned with the fee. It helped that I posted signs notifying customers of the fee, so they were aware of it going in. As a non-profit, this was fine at the time. However, since then things changed.

After the 2015 convention, Ohio changed their state laws for taxes and fees. As a result, it made a fee such as this questionable in the eyes of the state with regards to non-profits. Thankfully, that first year proved how much Authors Alley could contribute to the convention. The board waved the fee for upcoming years and dropped all prior ideas about charging authors participating in three or more panels.

Considering how difficult it can be to gauge whether funds will cover the costs of a convention, you often have to think outside the box to try and find solutions. Your situation will certainly be different in some ways, but it is essential to address the concerns of your panelists while maintaining solvency, especially of late with so many conventions going under. Please check your state's laws regarding taxes and fees before adopting this idea or a similar one.

Fighting Tradition

In the past, volunteers at conventions have contacted me expressing an interest in updating their literary departments. One of the difficulties they mentioned is the stubbornness of convention boards. They are often hesitant to change, especially in conventions that have been around for thirty years or more. As a result, I put together a slideshow explaining the essentials of how I created Cleveland ConCoction's Authors Alley and the results we saw over the first few years (available in Extras).

But why do literary departments need updated?

The publishing industry has changed tremendously since the development of e-readers and e-books. In fact, in 2008 e-book sales surpassed print sales. Since then the market has stabilized according to Lynn Neary (https://goo.gl/uuB63u) with NPR, but the modern publishing scene is far different from that of the '90s and earlier. Conventions with literary departments set up prior to 2000 are likely designed with traditionally published authors in mind. This can cause problems for author panelists who are self-published, have been published through independent small presses, or have published through a combination of methods like myself, called hybrid authors. Considering many traditionally published authors are now self-publishing or publishing through independent presses, according to Sabrina Ricci with IndieReader.com and the Huffington Post (https://goo.gl/5h5td8), conventions need to cater to all author panelists or the number of panelists will decline.

Pick Your Battles

As a department head of a convention, there are many things the board has to decide. In the case of fan-run conventions, every member is a volunteer. While every department head wants to create the best department possible, there is only so much time to go around. You don't want to irritate your co-workers or push them away.

If you have been involved in setting up conventions before, you probably know that you have to pick your battles. Everything can't be fixed at once, especially when a convention has been around for many years and may be used to doing things a certain way. Take it in stride and pick the most essential problems and/or policies to address and change each year. If something isn't addressed one year, try again the next. However, don't push too much. You want the support of your board.

I encountered some push back from people who said conventions weren't the place for writing conferences and large literary departments, but in the end increasing attendance proved them wrong. Thankfully these were not the feelings of the majority of volunteers at Cleveland ConCoction. Your situation will likely differ in a variety of ways, but if you have questions, feel free to contact me at weston@kincadefiction.com.

Book Sales

Conventions often do not allow authors to sell their books at autographing tables. Instead they require that authors purchase a table in the Vendors Hall (for a cost that is often more than authors can recoup), man it continuously throughout the convention (even though they have panels to attend, need to eat and use the facilities), or only allow authors to sell their books (if they allow sales outside the Vendors Hall at all) during the hour authors spend doing scheduled signings (which ultimately results in low to no sales). Alternatively, the author can place copies of their books on consignment with a book dealer in the Vendors Hall (which the vendor will expect to get up to 50 percent of the retail cost for each sale, leaving the author to take a loss on each book sold).

Book Vendors

While many conventions have book vendors that come and sell in the Vendors Hall, at Cleveland ConCoction we do not. The idea has been brought up, and I fully support book vendors and stores. However, for small and new conventions it is my opinion that such a vendor will actually hurt the sales of authors attending the convention. Although we have never had a book vendor at ConCoction, I believe authors who are participating in the convention should have priority over authors who aren't. While I respect their success and convention-goers' choice of reading material, their books can be purchased online and in many bookstores. Convention attendees interested in books are more interested in meeting participating authors, obtaining autographs, and attending panels and workshops. At ConCoction, we are open to publishers, editors, and authors of all genres. As the convention grows, we may pull in a book vendor, but for now it is not something I would recommend for small or new conventions due to the risk of our authors losing sales.

Competition

For the last few years there has been consistent competition from some commercial conventions, massive car shows, and even presidential speeches. You never know what will happen to draw people from your event; you just have to pick a date that will work best for your volunteers and convention fans.

Try not to overlap closely with other local conventions or large events. Competition can affect attendance and sales. However, authors who persist, actively sell, and network while at ConCoction still find that sales far outweigh the travel and hotel costs of the convention. As a department head, you can combat this drop in sales to some extent by making the convention as author and fan friendly as possible.

Convention Problems

With every event, there will be problems to deal with. In conventions these problems can run the gamut, from quite unique to mundane. At Cleveland ConCoction we've encountered some, but our experience has primarily been geared toward foreseeing problems before they occur and making arrangements to deal with them ahead of time. We try to be proactive, but we aren't always successful, and sometimes problems are simply unavoidable. The hotel will act accordingly to appease the guests who are staying, but that isn't everyone. The convention itself should also take steps to accommodate convention-goers if possible.

Most convention problems that you will deal with as an Authors Alley department head fall under the following categories:

- Facilities
- Panel Problems

Facilities

One of the biggest problems we encountered at Cleveland ConCoction has been parking. Over the last four years, lack of parking at the hotel, nearby airport construction, and widespread electrical outages have been major issues for convention attendees. The hotel was also sometimes overbooked, which created major problems for convention-goers. Some simply turned around and left when they couldn't find parking or could not get a room.

A second concern of high priority is facility space allocated for the convention. Depending on your location, some of this may be out of your control, but do your best to select facilities that will work well for your departments and provide enough parking arrangements for attendees, hotel guests, and volunteers.

Panel Problems

At every convention you sometimes encounter panelists or attendees that cause problems. For this reason, it is a very good idea to have a Code of Conduct posted online and physically (See Code of Conduct). The problems can be as blatant as something that violates the law or hotel rules and regulations. Normally Security or Operations handles such things, but what do you do when a convention-goer in one of your literary panels takes over the panel? More than likely, you won't be present during a situation like this and will only hear of it after the fact. Your panel moderator should handle this subtly, guiding the questions back to the topic at hand to regain control. If it is bad enough, when the Authors Alley gopher shows up, the moderator can alert them to the situation and either the Authors Alley department head or Security can be notified.

Sometimes the problem isn't an attendee though. Some panelists like to take this opportunity to advertise their books repeatedly, taking over the panel to an extent, which will annoy both attendees and other panelists. If you are alerted to this, it will probably be after the fact. At ConCoction, we have encountered this a couple times—not surprising considering how many author panelists we have participating each year. Each time I was notified when the convention was over, so the best solution was simply not to invite that author back in subsequent years. If I had been alerted to it earlier in the weekend, I would have pulled the author aside and carefully broached the topic. After the discussion, I would make sure they knew that if such actions continue they will not be welcome as a panelist in the future. Calm but stern discussions about the consequences of such actions will normally eliminate them from happening.

However, if it is something worse such as harassment, steps need to be taken to address the problem immediately. There have been many instances in the news and on social media over the last few years about conventions who have improperly dealt with these situations, and that kind of behavior is not to be tolerated from attendees or panelists. Security needs to be involved immediately, board members alerted to the problem, and likely the police. Each situation is different, but if other attendees' rights are being violated, the person responsible needs to be removed from the convention at the least and proper legal steps taken to address the wrong. People should not have to fear for their safety while attending a convention. Something like this requires that you also look to the future. Those actions are not welcome at family friendly conventions, and steps should be taken to ban them from future events. Rulings such as these are up to the convention board to decide though.

Conclusion

Thank you for reading *Build Your Authors Alley* and joining me on this convention journey. It has been fun and I've learned a lot, but the future is vast and full of the unknown. I am sure the unthinkable is on the horizon. Perhaps we will have a panel on that next year. Best of luck in your convention adventure. If you have questions or concerns not addressed within these pages, I can be contacted at weston@kincadefiction.com.

About the Author

Weston Kincade writes character-driven fantasy, paranormal, and horror novels that stretch the boundaries of imagination, and often genres. His current series include the Amazon bestselling A Life of Death trilogy and the Priors. Weston's thrilling short stories have been published in Alucard Press' "50 Shades of Slay," Kevin J. Kennedy's bestselling collections, and other suspenseful anthologies. He is a member of the Horror Writers Association (HWA) and helps invest in future writers while teaching. In his spare time Weston volunteers with Cleveland ConCoction's Authors Alley and enjoys spending time with his wife and Maine Coon cat, Hermes, who talks so much he must speak for the gods.

To find out more about Weston Kincade and Cleveland ConCoction, visit his website at kincadefiction.com and clevelandconcoction.org.

Extras

For your benefit, the examples mentioned throughout *Build Your Authors Alley* have been provided below along with links to the extras online.

Links

Email 1 – Convention Recruitment

https://goo.gl/o9Snbm

Email 2 – Convention Promotional Materials

https://goo.gl/TUAaW1

Email 3 – Panel Sign-Up

https://goo.gl/ioLYn3

Email 4 – Moderator's Responsibilities

https://goo.gl/KivHCw

Email 5 – Hotel Room Block

https://goo.gl/2dR9HC

Email 6 – Book Sales Announcement

https://goo.gl/vWgyCB

Final Panel Schedule

https://goo.gl/5G2tEY

Weekend Panel List

https://goo.gl/LkLSi6

Sales and Reimbursement Report

Build Your Authors Alley

https://goo.gl/weyhPE

Authors Alley Registration

https://goo.gl/BZGxJy

Authors Alley Newsletter

https://goo.gl/KeEmb8

Cleveland ConCoction Slideshow

https://goo.gl/ejRUUY

Authors Alley Email Examples

Please remember to change the email content relevant to your convention and personal signatures.

Email 1 – Convention Recruitment
Subject Headline: Invitation to Cleveland ConCoction

Hello there <<Name>>,
I'm organizing the Authors Alley for this year's Cleveland Concoction. Things have just started gearing up, and I'd like to officially invite you to attend as a guest author and panelist. As one of the only nonprofit conventions in Cleveland, Concoction is designed to appeal to a variety of genres. Our first two years of growth in attendance have shown that this is a prime location for such an event. This year's theme is In Space! The convention will take place March 11-13, 2016 at the Sheraton Hotel by the Cleveland Airport.

As an author myself, I understand the desire to have an author-friendly convention, and we're keeping that in mind as we organize Author Alley and our literary panels. Last year was a success, but we're working to improve it even more this year. To register with Cleveland ConCoction, complete and submit this form. Panel ideas are offered at the time of registration. Choose at least 3 that interest you. You can also submit ideas for any panels you don't see but would like to be involved in.

For more information, visit clevelandconcoction.org or feel free to ask. Melissa and I would be happy to answer any of your questions.

Happy reading and writing!

Email 2 – Convention Promotional Materials
Subject Headline: Materials Needed for Cleveland ConCoction

Hello <<Name>>,
I want to thank you once again for registering for Cleveland Concoction. We would like to start updating our website and flyers to highlight the authors we will be hosting this coming year. We should have your biographies and author photos from your registration, but could you send us anything else you might like included? We would like to promote any new books you have recently published. If you could send us a book cover image and a short description of each, we can promote these through our Facebook site. If you have anything upcoming that is not quite done, feel free to email us the details when you are ready!

We should be setting up the panel schedule soon. We pick the most popular panels from previous years and add some suggested panels to a schedule on SignUp.com, a free-access service. You will be assigned to those you chose when you originally registered that make the final cut and fall within your availability, but there will be plenty more to choose from. Look for the email in coming weeks.

Thanks again. Happy writing!

Build Your Authors Alley

Email 3 – Panel Sign-Up
Subject Headline: Panel Sign-Ups for Cleveland ConCoction

Hey there <<Name>>,
Wonderful news! Cleveland ConCoction's literary panels have been scheduled, and now you have the opportunity to pick any you'd like to join above and beyond the initial registration choices. New panels were added in some instances and some people had to be dropped from panels that wouldn't fit into their scheduled availability. Now's the time to make sure you are assigned to at least 3 panels, but please don't limit yourself. Have fun! All signups need to be completed by December 20th.

Here's how it works in 3 easy steps:
1. Click this link to go to our invitation page on SignUp.com.
2. Enter your email address. (You will NOT need to register an account on SignUp.com)
3. Sign up! Choose your spots. SignUp.com will send you an automated confirmation and reminders. Easy!
   Note: SignUp.com does not share your email address with anyone. If you prefer not to use your email address, please contact me and I can sign you up manually.

If you are a moderator for a panel, it is signified by (M). Your current convention panel schedule based on your initial interest is:
Shirley Crow
Friday 6-7pm Writing Cat Short Stories
Saturday 2-3pm Author Showcase (M)
Saturday 3-4pm Book Signing in Authors Alley
Sunday 10-11am Biggest Sins in Writing

Build Your Authors Alley

Additionally, if you haven't already, please email me your author photo, bio, and a very short description for each book we will be selling for you. (A couple sentences. Think Amazon advertising copy.)

If you have questions or concerns, please let us know. We look forward to seeing you at the convention. Happy writing!

Email 4 – Moderator's Responsibilities
Subject Headline: Attention Moderators

Hello again <<Name>>,

Thank you for joining us at Cleveland ConCoction this year. We look forward to having you as a moderator. In that vein, we thought an email highlighting the responsibilities of moderators would be beneficial.

Moderators at Cleveland ConCoction operate as experts in their field, panel guides, observers, and our immediate connection to the panel. To accomplish this, here are a few suggestions:

- To prepare for your panel, do a little research and prepare a list of 10 questions that will help guide the discussion, especially if conversation has meandered too far off topic.
- Remember to monitor the time. At 15 minutes before the hour, your panel needs to be concluded. This is to give attendees and panelists in the next scheduled panel time to find their seats, set up furniture, and also gives your guests time to make it to their next panel.
- Please count how many convention guests are in attendance at your panel and record that information on the sheet provided in your registration packet. This is to be returned to Authors Alley.
- If there are any concerns during your panel, let us know. We will be sending someone by to check on panel progress if you need anything.

For further advice, check out author Matt Moore's post on How to Be a Good Moderator (https://goo.gl/JTQQJd). If you have any questions or concerns, please let us know.

Email 5 – Hotel Room Block
Subject Headline: Hotel Room Block Reminder

Hey there <<Name>>,

The Cleveland ConCoction room block is still open. If you haven't booked (haha, puns) your hotel room yet, hurry before the deadline passes and rates go up. February 15th will be here before you know it, and the last thing we want is for you to be homeless over the weekend.

Here are the hotel rates for this year:

King rooms (one bed) are $81.00 per night
Queen rooms (two beds) are $89.00 per night
Oversized King rooms (one bed, but more space in the room) are $105.00 per night.
All above prices are subject to taxes and fees.

Call the hotel directly at 222-222-2222 and mention ConCoction to get the above rates, or go to http://hotelwebsite.com to reserve your room online.

We look forward to seeing you this year. Happy writing!

Build Your Authors Alley

Email 6 – Book Sales Announcement

Subject Headline: Cleveland ConCoction Sales Numbers

Hi <<Name>>,
It was wonderful having everyone at Cleveland ConCoction. Thank you for making this the best convention yet. Things seemed to go very well.

Here are the official numbers for book sales through the Author Alley Library. If you have any questions, please let me know at your earliest convenience. The checks will be sent out in the coming weeks. Your sales are given in the following format: Book Title, Number Sold, Value of Sales (rinse and repeat for each book), and then Total of all sales.

Book Title	Number Sold	Value of Sales	
Alabaster Dragons	3	$ 24.00	
Tampering with Ghosts	3	$ 24.00	
Criminal Minds and You	4	$ 40.00	Total: $ 88.00

Thanks and have a great year!

Authors Alley Newsletter Example

Authors Alley has started contacting guest authors for the upcoming Cleveland ConCoction 2018 convention, which will be March 9-11. So far we have over a dozen guest authors who plan to be part of Authors Alley and our panels during the weekend. Joining us so far are: JW Troemner, Olivia Berrier, Daniel A. Willis, Barbara Doran, J. Thorn, Addie J. King, Lucy A. Snyder, Sara Dobie Bauer, Linda Robertson, Marcus V. Calvert, Marie Vibbert, J.L. Gribble, Michael Timmins, Brent D. Seth, Cindy Matthews, Adrian Matthews, and Weston Kincade. We will be updating our website and social media to share our authors' biographies and descriptions of some of the publications they will be offering at the convention.

We would also like to hear about potential panel ideas for the next convention. Did you have some favorite panels you would like to see again? Do you have new ones you would like to suggest? Let us know via social media or email authors@clevelandconcoction.org.

We should be getting our upcoming Author Guest of Honor finalized soon, so pay attention to our social media sites. We look forward to seeing you at another outstanding convention in 2018!

www.ingramcontent.com/pod-product-compliance
Lightning Source LLC
Chambersburg PA
CBHW070207230526
45471CB00002B/854